All rights reserve

No portion of th

without written permission from the publisher or author, stored in a retrieval system, or transmitted, in any form by any means, including photocopying, recording, or other electronic or mechanical methods, without the prior permission of the author, the publisher except as permitted by U.S. copyright law.

To Evan:

Our imagination creates realities that don't yet exist.

Prologue

At the end of the day, it is not what we accumulate for ourselves but how much love, light, and kindness we give to others. It is about building others up and loving them wholeheartedly. Love is a perpetual well that never runs dry; we each have unique talents to reach our true potential.

From a young age, we're taught about the blue sky, the Earth's rotation, and why leaves are green. We learned to look both ways before crossing the street and to always be polite, honest, and kind. Through experiences, we've learned about love, pain, pleasure, and happiness. We grew through education, careers, and relationships, shaping our understanding of the world.

Life became an uphill battle: a quest for personal growth or simply avoiding failure. We juggled challenges, encountering negatives followed by positives. Along the way, we compared ourselves to others and made sense of our setbacks and triumphs relatively.

My story is no different. Like everyone else, I moved from one experience to the next, gaining wisdom and understanding. What I share here could be framed as a self-help essay, philosophical discussion, or yogic wisdom. However, this is simply a journey of observing, interpreting, understanding, and sharing insights about reality, our nature, time, consciousness, the Universe, and life.

This process required me to unlearn and relearn. Humbly, I share my findings, aware they're relative to my perspective and experiences. As Einstein once said, "Insanity is doing the same thing over and over again and expecting different results." A paradigm shift is necessary.

To the reader: This book is a guide. It will explore not just the theoretical but the practical steps toward transformation. By the end, you will have tools and exercises to manifest a fulfilled life, improve your mindset, and awaken your potential.

Chapter 1: The Awakening

It was a beautiful February morning. The sun shone brightly as I sipped a cup of coffee at the Bristol Hotel in Vienna. My watch read nine o'clock. I had just asked for a fresh newspaper. I hadn't read one in a while, but somehow, the act made me feel important. The setting was perfect - soaking up the sun, sipping coffee, and attempting to decipher German headlines. Then, a voice broke the stillness.

"We've got to hurry! Come with me!"

A well-dressed gentleman stood before my table, reaching out with urgency. Confused and cautious, I resisted. "I'm sorry, sir. I don't know you. What seems to be the matter?"

"The world as you know it is going to end! Haven't you read it in the paper?"

While I didn't trust him, I was curious. Was he dangerous or delusional? Still, something about his words resonated, as though he spoke to a part of me that knew what he meant. I decided to listen.

"You've been searching for truth your entire life," he said. "Every endeavor you pursued—wasn't it all in search of meaning?"

The stranger—Chris, as he introduced himself—seemed to know me better than I knew myself. He spoke of life as an illusion, a stage for experiences that help us grow and remember who we truly are.

"Whatever you think about manifests in your physical world," he explained. "When you think of calling someone, they often call you first. World events, circumstances—everything transforms to match the stream of your thoughts."

"Yes, but that's nothing out of the ordinary," I replied. "We often see only the things we want to see."

He smiled knowingly and sat down. "You've been searching for truth all your life. You've tried to find meaning in countless ways, haven't you?"

Discovering the Truth Within

Chris's words were startlingly accurate. He knew things about me—dreams, ambitions, and failures—that I had never shared with anyone. His insights shook my sense of reality.

"You once wanted to be a lawyer," he said. "Not because it was your calling, but because you thought it would make you feel important and accepted. Your true purpose lay elsewhere. We've been gently guiding you, ensuring you followed a path that aligns with your essence."

I was stunned. "Who are you? How do you know this?"

Chris leaned back, his expression calm but serious. "Everything is an illusion. The world as you perceive it is a game—a stage for transformation and growth. Humans often forget their true nature, becoming entangled in worldly desires and fears. But the truth has always been within you."

Lessons on Love and Connection

Chris spoke of love as the most powerful force in existence. "Humans seek external validation to fill internal voids," he said. "You desire power, acceptance, and security because you fear being incomplete. But genuine love—unconditional love—comes from recognizing your own wholeness. Every interaction should stem from a place of sincerity and compassion."

When I asked about war and human conflict, he replied, "These stem from self-hatred and fear. You hurt others because you feel incomplete. But remember: the world mirrors what you carry within. If you harbor jealousy or anger, you'll see it everywhere. If you cultivate love and kindness, the world will reflect that back to you."

A Call to Awaken

Chris urged me to reconnect with the purity and innocence of my inner self. "The world revolves around you," he said, "but to truly see it, you must return to your essence. Let go of attachments and live from a place of love. Life is a symphony; you're the composer. Choose your notes wisely, and you'll create something beautiful."

His words resonated deeply. I realized how often I'd lived in fear or sought external validation. Chris's insights challenged me to rethink my priorities and embrace a new perspective.

The Light Within

Our conversation shifted to the nature of existence. "Truth is," Chris said, "you are both the observer and the observed. The Creator and the Creation. Everything is interconnected. By peeling away layers of fear and attachment, you rediscover your true essence: pure, radiant love."

His final words stayed with me: "Remember, love transforms. Let it guide you, and you'll awaken to the infinite possibilities within and around you."

The awakening is not a destination but a journey—one that starts with a single step toward self-discovery.

Chapter 2: Observing Reality

At some point in our lives, all of us have wondered about the nature of reality. Why do we exist? What is the purpose of life? These profound questions often inspire a lifelong pursuit of truth. Humanity's hunger for understanding has driven science and philosophy, saving millions of lives and advancing civilization in countless ways. At the heart of this quest lies observation—the act of watching, reflecting, and connecting insights into meaningful wholes.

Observation is fundamental to every form of knowledge. By studying the world and its processes, we identify patterns, formulate hypotheses, and apply them in our daily lives. Through observation, we learn not only about others and the world but also about ourselves. Over time, our experiences shape our perspectives, beliefs, and thought processes. The ability to discern and interpret information is a vital skill that empowers us to navigate life more effectively.

The Power of Observation

Life is a series of learning experiences. Through observation, we make sense of the world, create new habits, and rebuild our understanding when necessary. This process is a delicate balance between logic and emotion, pleasure and pain. Duality is at the core of human existence, and it is through painful experiences that we often discover our strengths and capabilities. These moments challenge us to see ourselves in a new light, ultimately training our "muscles" to forge new paths to happiness.

The Role of Science and Religion

Both science and religion offer frameworks for understanding reality. While they may seem like opposites, they are two sides of the same coin—both striving to answer the fundamental questions of existence. Science relies on the systematic observation of phenomena to build knowledge, while religion often emphasizes surrender and faith to uncover deeper truths.

Consider the contributions of great minds like Newton, Einstein, and Curie. Their observations revolutionized our understanding of the physical world. Similarly, spiritual leaders like Jesus and Buddha taught us about the inner world—the realm of love, faith, and self-discovery. Despite their different approaches, these paths converge in their goal: to reveal the interconnectedness of all things.

The Parable of the Elephant

An ancient parable tells of three blind men encountering an elephant for the first time. Each touches a different part—the trunk, the tail, and the leg—and describes the elephant based on their limited experience. The moral of the story is that we often see what we expect or want to see, based on our subjective perspectives. To uncover the truth, we must expand our awareness and consider multiple viewpoints.

How to Cultivate Observation in Your Life

1. Practice Mindful Awareness:

Pay attention to the details of your daily life. Notice the colors, sounds, and sensations around you. This practice enhances your ability to observe and reflect.

2. Keep a Reflection Journal:

Each day, write down three observations about yourself, others, or the world. What did you notice? How did it make you feel?

3. Ask Questions:

Approach situations with curiosity. Instead of making assumptions, ask, "Why might this be happening?" or "What can I learn from this?"

4. Seek Diverse Perspectives:

Engage with people who have different beliefs or experiences. Their insights can challenge your assumptions and expand your understanding.

5. Embrace Humility:

Recognize the limits of your knowledge. Accept that there is always more to learn and observe.

Imagine you're in a disagreement with someone. Instead of reacting impulsively, step back and observe the situation. Ask yourself: What might they be feeling? What assumptions am I making? This reflective approach fosters empathy and opens the door to constructive dialogue.

The Truth Lies in Balance

Observation teaches us that truth often exists in the balance between extremes. Science and religion, logic and emotion, pain and pleasure—each offers valuable insights. By integrating these perspectives, we can develop a richer, more nuanced understanding of reality. The more we cultivate our ability to observe and reflect, the more we empower ourselves to live with clarity, purpose, and compassion.

Chapter 3: The Nature of Perception

Let us delve into the mechanisms that shape our understanding of the world: our senses. The human senses—sight, hearing, taste, smell, and touch—are the gateways through which we perceive and interact with reality. These sensory tools act as conduits, transforming vibrations and disturbances in the environment into signals the brain can interpret.

The eyes function as optical devices, capturing light and converting it into electrical signals that the brain processes into images. Similarly, the ears detect sound waves, the nose discerns chemical particles in the air, and the skin responds to pressure and temperature changes. These mechanisms allow us to navigate the physical world, yet their interpretations are inherently subjective, shaped by the limitations of human perception.

The Illusion of Density

While we perceive objects as solid and unyielding, the truth is far more complex. At the atomic level, matter is predominantly empty space. Atoms consist of a nucleus surrounded by electrons, with vast distances separating these components. The sensation of solidity arises from electromagnetic forces—opposing charges repelling one another. When you sit in a chair, for instance, you are not truly touching it. Instead, you experience the electromagnetic resistance that gives the illusion of contact.

This understanding reveals that much of what we perceive as tangible is an interpretation of sensory input, filtered and reconstructed by the brain to create a coherent experience of the world.

The Role of Consciousness in Perception

The brain does more than process raw data; it shapes reality through the lens of consciousness. Each individual processes information uniquely, based on their beliefs, experiences, and level of awareness. For example, two people might hear the same song but interpret its emotional tone differently, influenced by their memories and emotional states. This subjectivity highlights the intimate relationship between perception and consciousness.

Consider this: our sensory apparatus limits what we can perceive. We see only a narrow spectrum of light and hear a limited range of sound frequencies. Yet, the universe abounds with information beyond our physical senses—ultraviolet light, infrasound, and even subtle energetic fields. What we call "reality" is merely the fraction of existence that our senses can process, and our brain can interpret.

Why Can't We Walk Through Walls?

If atoms are mostly empty space, why can't we pass through solid objects? The answer lies in the electromagnetic forces that govern atomic interactions. The electrons in our body repel the electrons in a wall, creating a barrier that feels solid. This phenomenon illustrates how unseen forces shape our experience of the physical world.

To further understand this, imagine two magnets with the same poles facing each other. No matter how hard you push, the magnetic repulsion prevents them from touching. Similarly, the "solidity" we experience is a product of interactions at the atomic level, not an inherent property of matter.

Expanding Perception Beyond the Physical

While our physical senses provide a framework for navigating the world, they are not the sole means of perception. Practices like meditation, mindfulness, and introspection can help us access deeper levels of awareness. These practices allow us to perceive subtle realities, such as emotional energy, intuitive insights, and the interconnectedness of all things.

For instance, consider how you can sense someone's mood without them speaking a word. This "sixth sense" reflects our ability to perceive energy fields and emotional states, even if we cannot explain them scientifically.

Cultivating this awareness enhances our understanding of ourselves and others.

Practical Steps to Sharpen Perception

1. Engage Your Senses Fully:

Take time to focus on each sense individually. For example, during a meal, notice the flavors, textures, and aromas. This practice enhances your sensory awareness.

2. Practice Mindfulness:

Spend a few minutes each day observing your thoughts, emotions, and surroundings without judgment. This helps you become more attuned to subtle details.

3. Expand Your Sensory Boundaries:

Experiment with activities that challenge your perception, such as listening to different types of music, exploring nature, or practicing yoga. These experiences broaden your sensory and emotional range.

4. Meditate Regularly:

Meditation quiets the mind and enhances your ability to perceive beyond the physical senses. Focus on your breath and allow your awareness to expand inward and outward.

5. Cultivate Curiosity:

Ask questions about your experiences. Why does a sunset evoke awe? How does music stir emotion? Curiosity deepens your engagement with the world.

Our perception of reality is both a gift and a limitation. By understanding the mechanisms of our senses and exploring practices that expand our awareness, we can move beyond the surface of existence. This journey opens the door to a richer, more connected experience of life, allowing us to perceive the extraordinary within the ordinary. Through observation, mindfulness, and curiosity, we can uncover the deeper truths that shape our reality and transform our understanding of the world.

Chapter 4: Expanding the Boundaries of Awareness

The rate at which we process reality is limited by our five primary senses. Beyond the visible spectrum and audible frequencies lies an entirely different world—one that exists beyond the reach of our immediate perception. We interpret the world based on what we carry within us at any given moment. What we see, hear, and feel is filtered through our consciousness, shaped by our beliefs, experiences, and emotional states.

For instance, the visible spectrum of light that we perceive is just a tiny fraction of the electromagnetic spectrum. Similarly, our ears are attuned to specific sound frequencies, leaving vast realms of infrasound and ultrasound undetected. Yet, these unseen and unheard realities exist alongside us, influencing the world in ways we might never realize. If we could expand our perception, how much more of the universe could we understand?

The Filter of Consciousness

Human consciousness acts as a gatekeeper, filtering the overwhelming flood of information we encounter daily. Without this filtering mechanism, we would be inundated with sensory input, unable to process or make sense of our surroundings. However, this filtering comes at a cost: we miss much of the information available to us.

Imagine walking through a bustling city street. Your senses are bombarded with countless sights, sounds, and smells, yet your mind selectively focuses on a fraction of these stimuli. This selectivity allows you to navigate your environment effectively but also limits your awareness of the broader picture. By learning to quiet the mind and tune into subtle cues, we can begin to access the hidden layers of reality.

Breaking Free from Routine

Most of us live our lives on autopilot, following routines and distractions that keep us disconnected from our true selves. Over time, we lose touch with who we are and what we truly want. This disconnection makes us vulnerable to external influences—boredom, the need for validation, and fear.

When we let go of these distractions and reconnect with our inner selves, we gain clarity about our desires and purpose. We stop living for others' expectations and start living authentically. This shift requires courage, as it often involves confronting fears of failure, inadequacy, and pain. However, the rewards are immense: a life lived with intention, passion, and freedom.

Overcoming Fear and Embracing Love

Fear is one of the greatest barriers to expanding awareness. It keeps us trapped in cycles of doubt, insecurity, and avoidance. Yet, fear is often a product of our imagination—a projection of what might happen rather than what is.

Love, on the other hand, is the antidote to fear. When we approach life with love—toward ourselves, others, and the world—we dissolve the barriers that hold us back. This does not mean ignoring danger or taking unnecessary risks. Instead, it means allowing our hearts and souls to guide us, even when the path is uncertain.

Think of your life as a child you are raising. Would you neglect it or fail to nurture it? Of course not. Similarly, we must learn to love and care for our lives, embracing every experience as an opportunity for growth.

The Power of Presence

One of the most transformative practices for expanding awareness is cultivating presence. When we are fully present in the moment, we see beyond the surface of our experiences. We notice the subtle emotions, energies, and dynamics that shape our interactions.

For example, when someone acts out in anger, it often stems from their own pain and fear. By observing this with compassion rather than judgment, we can respond with understanding and kindness. This presence allows us to connect more deeply with others and with ourselves.

Steps to Expand Awareness

1. Declutter Your Mind:

Begin each day with a mindfulness practice, such as meditation or journaling, to clear mental distractions.

2. Question Your Beliefs:

Challenge assumptions and explore new perspectives. Ask yourself, "Is this belief serving my growth?

3. Seek Stillness:

Spend time in nature or quiet solitude, allowing yourself to tune into the rhythms of the world around you.

4. Practice Non-Attachment:

Let go of expectations and judgments. Accept experiences as they are, without clinging to outcomes.

5. Practice Unconditional Love:

Approach every interaction with love and acceptance. Recognize that everyone is on their own journey of self-discovery.

Expanding awareness is a journey of rediscovering the hidden depths within and around us. By breaking free from routine, overcoming fear, and cultivating presence, we can access new realms of understanding and connection. This path leads not only to personal growth but also to a greater sense of harmony with the universe. It is a reminder that we are more than we appear to be—boundless beings capable of perceiving and creating infinite possibilities.

Chapter 5: Understanding Our Essence

What is a soul or our essence? As with the existence of God, this has neither been scientifically proven nor disproven. Yet, we all sense that there is something deeper within us—a core essence that defines who we are. This essence is the driving force behind our actions and emotions, the unseen connector of our experiences and purpose.

The Birth of Awareness

When we are born, it is as though a switch is flipped. We are either alive or not; there is no in-between. Our perception of reality begins the moment that switch is turned on. In childhood, the world feels vast, time is irrelevant except for moments of intense longing, and our emotions are simple yet profound. We are either happy, hungry, or loved, and our emotional palette, while limited, feels limitless in intensity.

As we grow, our understanding of emotions becomes more nuanced. We learn to categorize, label, and navigate our feelings, shaped by our interactions and experiences.

While the core emotional states remain the same, our ability to partition and contextualize them evolves. For example, anger at a childhood toy being taken away transforms into frustration over an unmet goal as adults. The underlying emotion is familiar, but its triggers and expressions have matured.

The Role of Experiences in Shaping Our Worldview

Life is a series of interconnected experiences that shape our emotional and spiritual identity. Each interaction, whether joyous or painful, leaves an imprint on our soul. When we encounter a situation, our response is often dictated by past experiences, much like Pavlov's dogs responding to stimuli they were conditioned to recognize. For instance, think of the simple act of brewing coffee. For one person, it may evoke a sense of calm, rooted in memories of quiet mornings. For another, it might trigger stress, associated with hurried preparations for work. These associations, though seemingly small, are evidence of how our subconscious processes influence our emotions and reactions.

Taking Responsibility for Our Reactions

A vital aspect of understanding the essence is recognizing that we are the drivers of our emotional states. No matter the circumstances, we carry the power to choose our responses. It is not "Johnny," "Mary," or "Bob" who makes us angry, sad, or joyful. Rather, it is our interpretation of their actions and our internal narrative that dictates our emotional reaction.

This awareness is empowering. When we react with anger or resentment, we allow others to control our emotional state. However, when we respond with love, gratitude, or neutrality, we reclaim that control. Consider a disagreement with a friend. Reacting in anger might escalate the situation, but choosing patience and understanding can lead to resolution and growth.

The Impact of Emotional States on Life's Path

Our emotional responses shape the trajectory of our lives. Each decision, influenced by our emotional state, creates a ripple effect that impacts future opportunities and experiences. For example, persistent anger can close doors to meaningful relationships, while a consistent attitude of gratitude can open doors to unexpected blessings.

When we choose to operate from a state of balance and joy, we elevate the quality of our "tree of possibilities." This metaphorical tree represents the paths available to us at any moment. A tree nourished by positivity grows strong and abundant, offering countless fruitful branches. Conversely, one weighed down by negativity withers, limiting its potential.

Connecting with the Soul Through Self-Knowledge

To truly connect with our essence, we must first get to know ourselves deeper. This self-awareness allows us to navigate our emotions and align our actions with our inner truth. Think back to a time when you desired something deeply—a relationship, an achievement, or an object. Often, the desire was not for the thing itself but for the emotional state it represented. Understanding this connection helps us clarify our true needs and align with our soul's purpose.

Steps to Nurture the Soul

1. Practice Emotional Awareness:

Keep a journal to track your emotions and their triggers. Over time, patterns will emerge, helping you understand your emotional landscape.

2. Pause Before Reacting:

In moments of heightened emotion, take a deep breath and count to ten. This simple act creates space for intentional responses rather than reactive ones.

3. Cultivate Gratitude:

Start each day by listing three things you are grateful for. This practice shifts your focus to positivity and abundance.

4. Engage in Reflection:

Dedicate time to reflect on significant experiences, both positive and negative. Ask yourself: "What did this teach me about myself?"

5. Seek Balance:

Balance your mental, emotional, and physical well-being through activities like meditation, exercise, and meaningful conversations.

6. Connect with Nature:

Spend time outdoors, observing the interconnectedness of life. Nature has a way of reminding us of our place in the larger tapestry of existence.

Our Core Essence as our Guiding Light

Our essence is our internal compass, guiding us toward our highest potential. When we wrong someone or stray from our true path, the soul gently reminds us through feelings of guilt or discomfort. These moments are opportunities for growth, not condemnation. By being in tune with our core and aligning our actions with its guidance, we can live authentically and fully.

Understanding the soul is a journey of self-discovery. It requires patience, introspection, and a willingness to embrace both the light and shadow within us. By nurturing our soul and aligning with its wisdom, we unlock the ability to live to our maximum capacity—experiencing life not as a series of events but as a harmonious symphony of purpose, emotion, and connection.

Chapter 6: Understanding God and Our True Nature

Who is God, and what is his nature? Is he a figure cloaked in mystery—a wise old man with a flowing beard, perched on a celestial throne? Or is he something more profound, an essence that transcends all human conceptions? These questions have shaped the course of history and the paths of countless seekers.

The Personal Experience of God

Everyone's understanding of God is unique and deeply personal. Even the experience of disbelief is a relationship with the concept of God. Yet, one common thread persists: God is not confined by the structures of religion. Religion, in many ways, is a byproduct of humanity's quest to understand God, not the definition of Him.

One of my favorite physicists, Paul Dirac, once remarked, "God is a mathematician of a very high order, and He used advanced mathematics in constructing the universe." This insight points to a universe governed by intricate design and harmony, a reflection of divine intelligence.

Every moment of inspiration, every act of pure love and kindness, every time we feel peace and contentment in the simplicity of life—this is God manifesting within us. We can call Him by many names, but the truth remains: God is the light within us, the source of meaning, purpose, and inspiration. He is the gentle force that propels us forward when we feel we can no longer continue. He is the purity in our intentions, the grace in our actions, and the beauty in everything we perceive.

The Root of Suffering

Why do we suffer? At its core, suffering arises from forgetting our true nature. We become entangled in attachments—to people, experiences, and outcomes—mistaking them for sources of fulfillment. Suffering, however, is a construct, a product of our decisions and perspectives.

Imagine snapping your fingers and erasing all pain, leaving only perpetual joy. For a time, this state might seem perfect. Yet, soon, you would yearn for contrast, for challenge, for growth. This desire for variety, for the full range of experience, necessitates relinquishing some control. And in doing so, we encounter both joy and suffering.

Pain is not evidence of imperfection but a catalyst for remembering who we are. It teaches us to navigate the balance between our divine and human natures, to exercise our inherent goodness, and to master our emotions. Each instance of pain is an opportunity to refine our character and align closer with our true selves.

God Within Us

God is not a distant entity but a presence within each of us. It is the light that inspires, the love that connects, and the strength that sustains. This divine presence is evident when we act selflessly, when we forgive, and when we create beauty. It is the spark that guides us toward unity and wholeness.

Consider moments when you have felt deeply connected—to nature, to another, or to a higher purpose.

These experiences are glimpses of the divine within you. They remind us that we are both the Creator and the Creation, united in an infinite circle of being.

Steps to Connect with Divine Within:

1. Cultivate Stillness:

Spend time in quiet reflection or meditation. Allow yourself to feel the presence of divine within you.

2. Embrace Gratitude:

Acknowledge the blessings in your life. Gratitude opens the heart to divine abundance.

3. Act with Love:

Approach every interaction with kindness and compassion. In doing so, you reflect divine love.

4. Surrender Control:

Let go of the need to dictate outcomes. Trust in the divine flow of life.

5. Seek Meaning in Painful Experiences:

Instead of resisting pain, ask what it is teaching you. Use it as a pathway to growth.

6. Celebrate Beauty:

Recognize the divine in the world around you—in art, nature, and the small miracles of daily life.

The Balance Between Human and Divine Nature

Life is a delicate dance between our human vulnerabilities and our divine potential. Experiences, whether joyful or painful, allow us to explore this balance. By embracing both sides of our nature, we discover the depth of our capacity for love, creativity, and resilience.

Each person we encounter and every challenge we face serves as a mirror, reflecting aspects of ourselves that need growth or acceptance. This interconnectedness reminds us that we are never alone; we are part of a greater whole, a symphony of divine expression.

God is not a concept to be understood but an essence to be experienced. It is the love that unites us, the wisdom that guides us, and the light that illuminates our path. By recognizing this presence within and around us, we align with our true nature and embrace the fullness of life. Through this journey, we remember that we are both human and divine, and in this unity, we find our purpose and peace.

Chapter 7: The Observer's Role in Reality

The world and reality, as we perceive them, are deeply rooted in observer-oriented experiences. Each of us plays two roles simultaneously: the actor who participates in life and the executor who influences outcomes. This duality forms the fabric of our existence, where our perspective shapes how the stage of life unfolds.

The Illusion of the Stage and Time

Reality often feels like a grand stage, complete with characters, plotlines, and props. Time, as we experience it, appears to flow in a linear fashion, creating a sense of continuity. Yet, these are merely illusions, constructs of the mind to help us navigate existence. Everything we do, every experience we engage in, revolves around us—the observer.

However, not all paths we tread align with our true calling. When we stray from this alignment, we create possibility trees that lead to unproductive outcomes, steering us away from our fullest potential. The quality of our experiences and the emotions we nurture play a pivotal role in maintaining harmony with our true self.

The Reflective Nature of Experiences

Every person we meet and every challenge we face acts as a mirror, reflecting aspects of ourselves that require growth or understanding. These reflections illuminate the areas that need refinement. We have the power to choose how we interact with these reflections: from a place of love or anger, compassion or fear.

For instance, consider a situation where someone criticizes you. Do you react defensively, or do you take a moment to reflect on what this interaction reveals about your insecurities or strengths? By choosing love and understanding, we transform every experience into a stepping stone toward self-mastery.

Polishing Our Edges

Life is an intricate process of learning and growth. Each experience, whether joyful or painful, polishes our edges, making us more attuned to our higher self. The more in touch we are with our inner truth, the purer our intentions become. This purity aligns us with a more abundant tree of possibilities, filled with outcomes that resonate with our true purpose.

To achieve this, sincerity is key. Trusting ourselves and embracing honesty in our intentions clears the path for authentic growth. This process is not about perfection but about progression—a journey of becoming more aligned with the core essence of who we are.

The Unified Matrix of Existence

We weave our own matrix of existence, an embroidery where all is interconnected. Time, as we perceive it, is an illusion. Everything happens simultaneously; each moment, each iteration, coexists in the infinite now. The separateness we experience is relative, a necessary construct to help us focus on individual journeys.

Picture a tree with countless branches, each representing a unique life or experience. While the branches appear distinct, they all stem from the same trunk, the same source. This interconnectedness reminds us that we are both the creator and the creation, self-discovering and self-observing through the myriad patterns of existence.

Steps to Embrace Observer-Centric Reality

1. Reflect on Experiences:

After significant events, take time to journal or meditate. Ask yourself, "What did I learn from this? What does it reveal about me?"

2. Cultivate Emotional Awareness:

Before reacting to situations, pause and identify the emotions you feel. Are they rooted in fear or love?

3. Align with Your True Calling:

Regularly revisit your goals and aspirations. Are your actions moving you closer to your authentic self?

4. Practice Gratitude:

Acknowledge the people and experiences that challenge you. They are opportunities for growth.

5. Engage in Mindful Observation:
Spend time observing your surroundings without judgment. Notice the interconnectedness of everything.

The observer's role in shaping reality is profound. By recognizing our dual role as both actor and executor, we reclaim the power to influence our experiences. Through reflection, sincerity, and alignment with our true self, we can navigate life's stage with grace and purpose. This journey is not about control but about harmony— embracing the interconnectedness of existence and the infinite possibilities it holds.

Chapter 8: The Observer as the Creator of Reality

The observer is not just a passive participant in the physical world but the maker of reality itself. Every aspect of the physical world, as we perceive it, is a transformation projected by consciousness. Through this lens, our experiences are shaped, guided, and interpreted by the interplay of perception and intention.

Reality as a Projection

Each individual consciousness acts as the driver of its own reality, operating within a unique matrix of perception. This matrix is a projection—a dynamic, ever-changing representation of information tailored to our awareness. Within this framework, obscurations or the limitations of perception, influence what we see and how we interpret the world.

Consciousness behaves like a prism, transforming and scattering information into patterns that form the illusion that we perceive as physical reality. This phenomenon, which I call coalescence, involves threading and weaving disparate pieces of information into a cohesive narrative.

Perspectival relativity—the way each observer perceives reality—depends on the rate at which we process information and our level of awareness.

Threading the Needle of Perception

Human consciousness can be likened to a metaphorical needle threading through layers of information. These layers, much like musical notes on a staff, contain the building blocks of experience. By "threading the needle," we connect these layers to form a cohesive pattern, creating the illusion of causality and continuity.

For example, consider the experience of watching a movie. Each frame is a static image, but when played in rapid succession, the brain perceives motion and flow. Similarly, consciousness stitches together moments of existence, creating the perception of a seamless, flowing reality.

The Illusion of Time and Space

Time and space, as we understand them, are constructs designed to make reality manageable. Our senses act as gates, slowing down the overwhelming flood of information to create the illusion of sequential experiences. This "slowdown" is essential for us to process, interact with, and transform the world around us. Imagine a video game. To make the game playable, the system separates and channels vast amounts of information into digestible fragments for the player. Similarly, our sensory apparatus filters and organizes information, providing a usable framework for living in the physical world.

The Playground of Creation

The physical world can be seen as a playground where we, as observers, weave the threads of reality. Within this plane, we create intertwined patterns and ornaments, each representing a unique expression of our consciousness. Until we focus on a specific "note" or intention, the possibilities remain infinite. Human consciousness selects, transforms, and builds experiences from this homogenous pool of potential.

This means that the possibilities are limitless. Depending on our level of awareness, processing speed, and affective state, we are the ultimate makers of the experience of reality.

Practical Applications for Shaping Reality

1. Set Clear Intentions:

Define what you wish to create in your life. Focus your thoughts and actions on aligning with this vision.

2. Embrace Flexibility:

Understand that reality is fluid. Be open to changes and unexpected opportunities that align with your intentions. Remember the dynamic nature of self, allow the self to go with the flow.

3. Practice Visualization:

Regularly visualize the outcomes you desire. Notice how it makes you feel, what emotional state associates with this. This exercise strengthens the connection between your consciousness and the reality you wish to create.

4. Engage in Mindful Observation:

Pay attention to the details of your experiences. Notice patterns and synchronicities that guide your path.

5. Trust the Process:

Let go of the need to control every aspect of your reality. Trust that your essence.

As observers, we hold the profound ability to shape and create our reality. By understanding the mechanisms of perception and intention, we unlock the power to transform our experiences. This journey of creation is both an individual and collective quest, reminding us of the infinite possibilities within the matrix of existence. Through mindfulness, intention, and trust, we become architects of our own lives, creating the leitmotif of reality with purpose and grace.

Chapter 9: Non-Attachment and the Art of Being

While human life is rich with emotional states, there is one state that holds transformative power: the state of non-attachment. This state allows us to simply be—to observe life without judgment and without clinging to outcomes. Non-attachment is not apathy but a profound acceptance of reality as it is.

The Essence of Non-Attachment

Non-attachment invites us to let go of labels and roles. You are not defined by your successes or failures, nor by what you have or lack. Instead, you exist in a state of equilibrium, where the mind, body, and soul align. In this state, you accept yourself as you are—perfect, loved, and whole.

When we let go of unresourceful thoughts and meet ourselves without fear, we discover our true essence. This is the space where transformation begins. Non-attachment is the key to unlocking the deeper layers of our being.

Tracing Fear to Its Source

Fear often anchors us to the illusion of control. To practice non-attachment, start by tracing your fears to their root. For example, if you fear not receiving a promotion, ask yourself:

- What happens if I don't get it?
- What is the worst-case scenario?
- How would that outcome make me feel?
- How can this push me out of my comfort zone?
- What does this teach me?

Instead of focusing on the physical outcome, explore the emotional states underlying your fear. Identify whether these emotions stem from rejection, insecurity, or a fear of failure. By bringing these feelings into awareness, you begin to disarm their hold on you.

The Practice of Letting Go

Once you've identified the emotions, allow yourself to fully feel them. Sit with the discomfort without judgment.

Notice that while these feelings may be intense, they are temporary—like clouds passing through a sky. Recognize your strength in enduring them and let them dissipate naturally.

As you practice this, you'll notice that the castles of fear and anger you've built begin to crumble. The situations that once triggered you lose their power, and you become free to respond from a place of love and calm. Perhaps, any given situation helps you to reassess your current state and unlocks new opportunities for you.

Building a Life of Non-Attachment

1. Daily Reflection:

At the end of each day, reflect on moments where you felt attached to outcomes. Journal about these experiences and consider how you might approach them differently.

2. Mindful Meditation:

Practice mindfulness by observing your thoughts without engaging with them. Let them come and go, like waves on a shore.

3. Embrace Impermanence:

Remind yourself that everything in life is transient. Cherish the present moment without clinging to it.

4. Focus on Intentions, Not Results:

Shift your mindset from outcome-driven to intention-driven. Instead of striving for a specific result, focus on the quality of your actions and the authenticity of your intentions.

5. Cultivate Gratitude:

Gratitude grounds us in the present. By appreciating what we have, we reduce our attachment to what we think we lack.

Non-attachment is a state of liberation, where we are no longer bound by fear, anger, or the need to control. By embracing this state, we align with our true selves, experiencing life with clarity and grace. Each moment becomes an opportunity to connect deeply with the essence of who we are and to navigate the world with love and freedom.

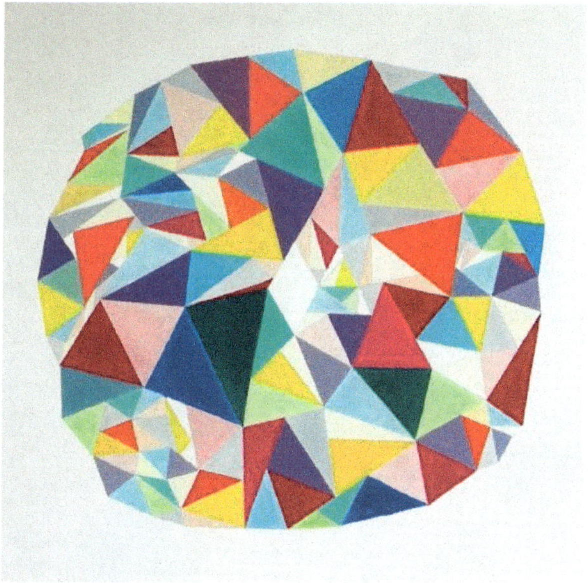

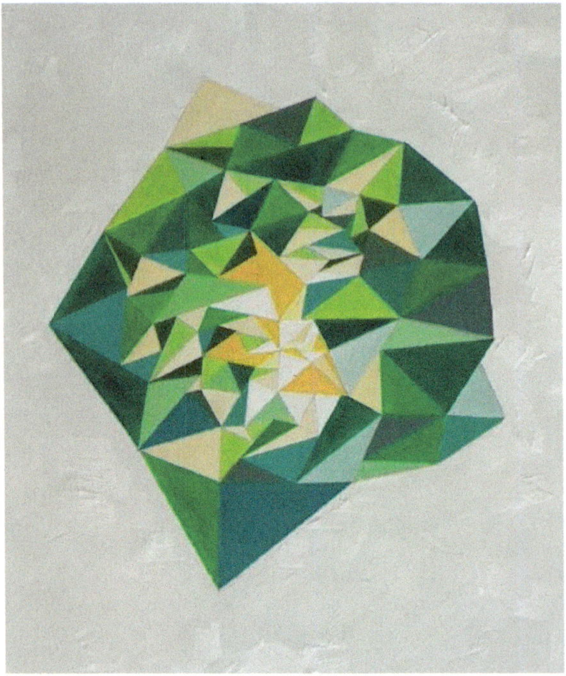

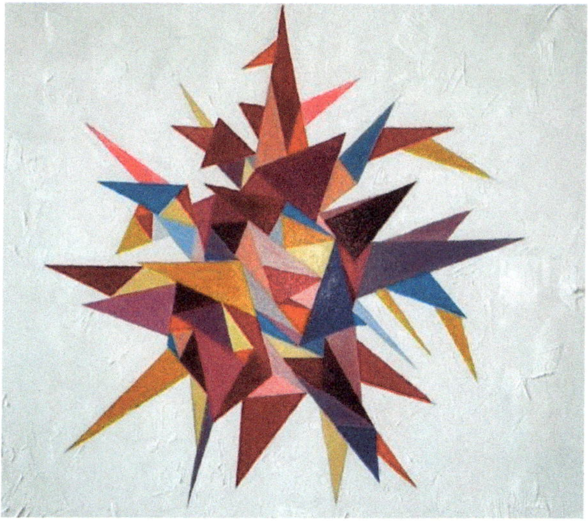

Wishing you much love and light on your journey to self-discovery.

Made in the USA
Las Vegas, NV
14 February 2025